I0539153

THE BAYOU BOUNCE

BOOK ONE
RESILIENCE
WRITTEN BY
TYAISHA DILLON

ILLUSTRATED BY
RANDELL PEARSON

Copyright © 2025 by Tyaisha Blount-Dillon
Printed in the United States of America
Published in Hellertown, PA

All rights reserved. No part of this publication may be reproduced or transmitted in any form or by any means,
electronic or mechanical, including photocopying, recording, or any other information storage and retrieval system,
without the written permission of the author or publisher.
Internet addresses given in this book were accurate at the time it went to press.

This book is a work of fiction. All of the names, characters, events, and incidents in this book are
a product of the author's imagination. Any resemblance to actual persons or events is purely coincidental
and not intentional. If long-standing institutions, agencies, public buildings, and geographical locations
are mentioned, the characters and events surrounding them are wholly imaginary.

This work is the property of the author and should not be distributed without the author's permission.

ISBN 979-8-89420-060-6
Library of Congress Control Number: 2025916101

The Bayou Bounce by Tyaisha Dillon
Illustrations and Book Design by Randell Pearson, Pearson Designs
The text of this book is set in Minion Pro

First printing edition 2025

For more information or to place bulk orders, contact the author or the publisher at
Jennifer@BrightCommunications.net

Bright
COMMUNICATIONS

*To my family and to everyone
quietly struggling with Parkinson's*

OUR HOME

Hi! I'm Will, and I'm nine years old. Laughter, music, and the delicious aromas from our kitchen make my home a joyful place to live. My household includes my mom, my dad, our dog Roman the "Rotti," and me! My family is from Louisiana, but we live in Georgia now. I love the Saints and Southern University! I enjoy playing football, making stop-motion movies, and rocking out on my electric guitar. My biggest fans? Mom and Dad, of course!

Draw a picture of your home and the people (and pets) who make it feel special.
What's something you love doing at home that always makes you happy?

MEET MOM

My mom is amazing! She's from Baton Rouge, the "Red Stick." She's like the Louisiana sun: warm, strong, and shining—even on tough days. She rocks different hairstyles, just like she rocks life. Mom fills our home with music, joy, and yummy smells.

She also has some pretty cool stories from her past. Although she is from Baton Rouge, home of the LSU Tigers, she only talks about the University of Tennessee because that is where she got her master's degree in Biosystems Engineering Technology. Mom also worked at the state capitol with a local senator and his staff! She got to see how local government works up close—and even pressed the button to vote on bills when the senator had to step away!

Do you know someone with an interesting job or life story, kind of like my mom?
Draw or write about what they do and why you look up to them.

MEET DAD

Dad is from Baton Rouge too! He is a soil scientist, and he loves to fish, hunt, and cook. He even cooks gumbo better than Mom! You must read Book Two to learn more about my outdoor adventures with Dad!

Dad enjoys taking me with him when he goes fishing. At first, I didn't understand why we had to sit there for so long, waiting for a fish to bite. "This is boring, Dad," I said.

"Fishing isn't just about catching fish, Will. It's about patience. Sometimes, the fish don't bite, but that doesn't mean the time isn't worth it," Dad said.

As we sat there, Dad taught me that nature can be relaxing. The water and ripples have a rhythm. If you try to match your heartbeat to the rhythm of the waves, you will start to feel calm.

"When you rush, you miss the best parts of life," Dad said, casting his line again. I looked at him and realized that fishing was not only about catching fish. It also teaches me to practice patience, which is hard for me because I'm a kid!

When I finally caught my first fish, I was so proud, and Dad said, "That was good, Will. But remember, the best catches don't always come quickly; they come when you're ready."

Think about someone in your life who has taught you something important. What did you learn from them? You can write about it or draw a picture.

OUR TRADITIONS

In Louisiana, we have many traditions. One of my favorites is Mardi Gras. Every year, my parents attend a Mardi Gras ball in Atlanta. Mom loves to attend because the ball benefits an all-boy's school in New Orleans. Mom usually wears a dress with shiny things on it, and Dad wears a tuxedo. This year, Mom is worried because she must decorate an umbrella for the second line, and the umbrella she ordered has not arrived.

The second line is like a parade, and it's an example of pure showmanship. These parades are often held to mourn the passing of a person or to celebrate an event, like a wedding. Usually a brass band plays, and people walk and dance in the line.

Does your family have a fun tradition or celebration?
Draw or write about what makes it special and how you celebrate it together.

THE KITCHEN IS COMMUNITY

Our house is always alive with music and friends. In the morning, the aroma of Community Coffee fills the house. It's Mom's favorite, and it's made in Port Allen, Louisiana!

In Louisiana, families gather in the kitchen to cook, share stories, and pass down recipes. Mom and Dad enjoy playing the radio-edited versions of Big Freedia, Trombone Shorty, and the Rebirth Brass Band. They really love Zydeco, Bounce, and any other type of music that has Louisiana roots. Oh yes and radio-edited means good music, minus the bad words!

While Mom cooks, she starts a call-and-response.

"Add the seasoning! Add the spice!" I join in, marching around the kitchen as she chuckles.

Make up a call-and-response song!

MOM'S DANCE

My mom has young-onset Parkinson's disease, which affects how she moves. Sometimes her movements slow down, or she deals with painful stiffness called dystonia. Dystonia can be described as muscle rigidity or stiffness, and Mom says they are like horrible, painful muscle cramps. Even so, she is strong, and she faces every day with grace and determination.

It took years for Mom's doctors to figure out what was wrong, but Mom never gave up. She told me it was like solving a puzzle without having all the pieces. She saw so many doctors— more than I can count— until she found one who listened to her. That doctor helped her start a treatment that would help her feel better. My mom is a success again on the dance floor, in the board room, and beyond!

If you were a doctor meeting someone like mom, how would you help her feel like you understand what she's going through and that you really care about her?

MOM'S SECRET INGREDIENT FOR MOVING

Mom says to think of her like a beignet—a fried pastry made of leavened dough, cut into squares, and dusted with powdered sugar. In Mom's case, the sugar is a neurotransmitter called dopamine. *Neuro* means nerves or the nervous system, which is a complex network that controls your actions by transmitting signals to and from different parts of your body. Without dopamine, or powdered sugar, messages do not get from Mom's brain to her body.

Mom had a special surgery to place two tiny implants in her brain that send steady electrical signals to the front of her brain and help her move better. The doctors don't exactly know how the technology works. But Mom's implants help her feel stronger and more in control!

Mom's recovery taught me something important: Everyone has the power to be strong. You can build strength with positive thoughts you put into action. For example, when I struggled with reading because of my dyslexia, I wanted to give up. I thought, *If Mom can be strong, I can keep trying too.*

One day, I brought a book home from school. "I'm going to read this to you, even if it takes all night," I told Mom.

She smiled and said, "Take your time, Will. You've got this."

Imagine your favorite food has a secret ingredient that gives you energy, focus, or strength. Draw the food and label the secret ingredient.

SELF-IMPROVEMENT

Mom talks about self-improvement a lot. She even took dance classes to help improve her movement. I'm not a fan, but she loves it. Mom comes home from her classes happy, boasting her Apple watch recorded she burned 500 calories.

She has a cool app on her watch. It allows doctors to adjust patients' treatments more accurately based on real-time data of symptoms. Mom developed a plan to improve her health. It included juicing green vegetables to feel stronger, staying active through dancing and cycling, and stretching every day—even on tough days.

"When life gets hard, don't sit still—move!" Mom says. That's why she dances, cycles, and stretches every day.

I once asked her, "Why do you work so hard, Mom?"

She smiled and said, "Because every healthy choice I make helps me win against Parkinson's, and I want to keep dancing with you for a long time."

What would you say to someone who needs help? Write or draw how you would encourage them!

PARKINSON'S AND ZYDECO

Mom is fond of Zydeco music, which is a lively, unique blend often heard at festivals, dance halls, and family gatherings. Zydeco is a type of music that makes you want to move your feet. It mixes accordions, washboards, and upbeat rhythms to create a happy, fast-moving sound. I believe a Zydeco dance class could be amazing therapy for her and other Parkinson's patients. The upbeat rhythms and energetic movements might help ease their rigidity and get them moving more freely. What I love most about Zydeco is its deep connection to the community. It brings people together.

Make up your own dance to Zydeco music or draw a dance move that makes you feel strong.

21

COOKING WITH DAD

One day, Dad decided it was time for me to learn how to cook. "Cooking is just like life," he said as we stood in the kitchen. "Measure your ingredients carefully, just like you measure your time and effort." We made jambalaya together.Dad chopped the vegetables and showed me how to stir the pot just right.

"This is the trinity of cooking in Louisiana. We use onions, celery, and bell peppers," my dad said. "You can't make good jambalaya without them." I chopped the vegetables with care, trying not to cut them too big or small.

"Just like in football, it's about working as a team. In cooking, every ingredient plays a role," Dad said. As we worked, Dad told me that cooking, like fishing and football, is about patience and practice.

"You're going to make mistakes, Will, but you'll learn from them. And when you get it right, it'll taste even better." The jambalaya we made was delicious, and I felt proud to be part of the family tradition.

Write about a time when you had to work as a team and describe the different responsibilities you had.

LEARNING FROM THE TOUGH DAYS

Sometimes Mom has appointments with the neurologist, and she can't take her Parkinson's medication. The day before, she'll say, "Will, I won't be able to help much tomorrow, so please complete all your tasks."

"No worries, Mom. I got this!"

"Thank you, Will. You're a good kid. Will, today's one of my tough days. We all have them. It's like the trinity. Onions, bell peppers, and celery give each dish its flavor. Likewise, with each challenge we face, every ingredient adds something unique to who we are. They give us our flavor!"

One day, I was getting frustrated with archery practice. Every time I shot the bow, the arrow missed the target. I got upset. "I'll never get it, Dad!" I groaned.

Dad came over and put his hand on my shoulder. "Will, frustration is part of the process. You won't always hit the bullseye right away. But you must keep practicing and stay patient with yourself."

He showed me how to breathe deeply before shooting, how to aim carefully, and how to steady my hands. "You see, archery is about focus and control. The more you practice, the better you get, even if you miss a few times."

After several tries, I hit the target, not perfectly, but enough to make me smile. "See? We make progress one shot at a time," Dad said.

What do you do when you get frustrated? Write a tip that helps you stay calm and keep trying!

25

DOING THE RESEARCH

Mom is a Research Advocate for Parkinson's. She believes there is power in your voice. You will rarely hear her expressing any negative thoughts. One of the most impressive parts of Mom's journey was when she transformed from a person who was almost disabled into a mobile, fit person with a voice!

Now, Mom advocates for the changes she wants in her health care. She uses her voice to help others who want her help. She works countless hours assisting a pharmaceutical company in developing programs to give people of color access to genetic testing and clinical trials.

I think Mom works so hard because she doesn't want me or anyone else to suffer from Parkinson's. Mom says genetic testing gives patients power because it helps doctors develop treatments designed for us.

Imagine you're a health detective like my mom. What question would you ask a doctor or scientist to learn how to help people with Parkinson's disease? Draw yourself with the question in a speech bubble.

DANCING WITH MOM

Mom's dance is beautiful and inspiring, and I'm proud to be her dance partner. When I dance with her, I feel strong and happy. Mom's rhythm might be unique, but she owns it—and that makes her dance perfect. You may laugh, but dance could help you in football. My granddad played football in college and was required to take a dance class.

Every time I step onto the football field, I think about everything that I was taught. "Football isn't just about winning," he always said. "It's about teamwork, effort, and never giving up."

We practiced in the backyard after school, throwing the ball back and forth. Dad showed me how to hold it correctly, how to throw a spiral, and how to always keep my eyes on the target. "Just like in life, you need to stay focused and follow through, even when things don't go as planned," he said.

One day, I fumbled the ball, and Dad said, "It's okay to make mistakes, Will. What matters is what you do next. Get up, shake it off, and try again."

We practiced that afternoon for hours, and by the end, I was throwing passes like a pro. Dad smiled and said, "That's the spirit. Keep practicing, and you'll keep getting better."

Create your power dance move—a bounce, spin, clap, or step that makes you feel strong and happy. Show it to someone and try it together. How did that make you feel?

THE BEAT OF MOM'S ADVOCACY

Parkinson's makes some things harder for Mom, but she always gets through it because she is determined. Mom has even fiercely advocated for me too, and she encourages me to do the same for myself. Mom must put that type of effort into her wellness. Just as Dad must add all those ingredients to make his dish, Mom carefully selected her care team to include an athletic trainer, mental health provider, nutritionist, and doctors. Building a team takes time, but it's worth it.

Mom's brain surgery was like planting a seed in tough soil. At first, it didn't look like much was happening. But with care, sunlight, and time, something amazing grew. I noticed she spent more time talking about helping other people. She wasn't just focused on getting stronger for herself; she wanted to make a difference for everyone who faced struggles like hers.

One afternoon, I found Mom at the kitchen table with her laptop and surrounded by papers, and I asked, "What are you working on, Mom?"

"I'm writing a letter to a group that helps people like me get genetic testing," she explained. "There are so many people who don't know they can get help because they've never been told about it. I want to change that."

ADVOCACY REFLECTION

Mom told me some people in our community knew little about the connection between their health problems and their family history. She explained how understanding their genes could help doctors find better treatments, just like the ones that helped her.

Mom shared our story with others so they could understand their health better. She said, "Learning more about my genes helped me and my family. It could help you and yours too." That day, I saw how Mom's recovery wasn't just about healing her body. It showed me how to tackle my challenges too. "This isn't just about science," Mom said. "It's about giving people the chance to feel hopeful."

When I struggled with math or reading, I thought about how Mom kept moving forward, no matter how tired she was.

One day, after a tough week at school, I told her, "I don't think I'm good at reading, Mom."

"Will, you can do anything if you keep practicing. Remember how I couldn't even walk to the mailbox? Now I'm running around the neighborhood." Those words stayed with me. They made me believe hard work could help me, just like it helped her.

Everyone has their unique rhythm, just like my mom.

YOU CAN DANCE TOO!

The End

GLOSSARY

DEEP BRAIN STIMULATOR: A tiny medical device that works kind of like a light switch in the brain. Doctors put it in carefully to send gentle signals that help the brain and body move more smoothly, almost like music helping a dancer keep rhythm.

DOPAMINE (DOH-puh-meen): A chemical in the brain that helps send messages to the body to move.

DYSTONIA (dis-TOH-nee-uh): Painful muscle cramps caused by Parkinson's disease.

NEUROLOGIST (new-ROL-uh-jist): A doctor who helps with the brain and nerves.

PARKINSON'S DISEASE (PAR·kuhn·snz): A progressive neurological disorder that primarily affects movement that develops due to the degeneration of nerve cells in the brain, specifically those that produce dopamine, a neurotransmitter crucial for motor control.

RESILIENCE (rih-ZIL-yuhns): Being strong and bouncing back, even when life is tough.

TRINITY: A special mix of onions, celery, and bell peppers that makes Louisiana food taste amazing.

YOUNG-ONSET PARKINSON'S DISEASE: A kind of Parkinson's disease that shows up in adults much earlier than usual, even when they're still young parents. It makes moving harder, but with treatment, exercise, and support, people can still dance, smile, and enjoy life.

ZYDECO (ZAI-duh-koh): Music that comes from an eclectic blend of musical cultures, including Creole, and rhythm and blues from African American communities. Instruments used are items you can find around the house or items you could find around your great-grandparent's house, such as a spoon or a washboard. Other instruments include the drums and the accordion.

Special thanks to

Black Health CAB

Anita Parker

Hiral G. Shah, MD, and family

ABOUT THE AUTHOR

TYAISHA BLOUNT-DILLON is a passionate advocate for brain health, a nationally recognized environmental leader, and according to her son, a real-life superhero. But in truth, he is the real hero—because his love, curiosity, and keen observations inspired doctors to finally give her the correct diagnosis after more than a decade of uncertainty.

Tyaisha has been living with young-onset Parkinson's disease for 25 years, and she's transformed that personal journey into a powerful mission to help other families thrive. With more than 16 years of leadership in federal government programs, she's created initiatives that protect the planet, educate youth, and empower communities. Today, she leads The Thriving Brain & Development Project Inc., where she works alongside partners like Aetna, Chef Traci Vincent, Columbia University, and The SAE School to deliver innovative programs in brain health, nutrition, and environmental justice.

Tyaisha is developing NeuroSeeds, a one-of-a-kind education and wellness program that helps children and families grow strong minds and healthy bodies. She has been honored by the HollyRod Foundation, was featured in a national Parkinson's Foundation commercial, and proudly serves as a Parkinson's Foundation Research Advocate. She has served the required time as a member of the Patient Advisory Board and Udall Foundation.

Whether she's volunteering, facilitating cooking events, or writing books that will encourage kids to pursue careers in science or health, Tyaisha's greatest inspiration is her family—her son and husband, whose compassion and strength helped motivate her path to healing.

She lives in Georgia with her husband and son and believes that when we lead with love and I earning, anything is possible—especially when we plant seeds of brain health literacy to grow stronger minds and brighter futures.

ABOUT THE ILLUSTRATOR

RANDELL PEARSON is an independent illustrator and graphic designer with over five decades of professional experience in both the corporate and private sectors. ■ He attended The High School of Art and Design (NYC), Hunter College (CUNY), The School of Visual Arts (NYC) and, Stanford University (Palo Alto, CA). Randell has garnered awards from the Art Directors Club of New York, The Society of Illustrators (NYC), The Type Directors Club (NYC) and, The Society of Publication Designers (NYC). ■ His work has been exhibited at the Brooklyn Museum of Art, and Parke - Bernet Galleries (NYC). He has received special recognition from the late Coretta Scott King, actress Jane Fonda, veteran NY1 Spectrum News Anchor Cheryl Wills and *America's Cup* winning sailor and, businessman Bill Koch, to name just a few of the many notable individuals who have appreciated his work. In a related Parkinson's project, Randell illustrated and designed the highly acclaimed *PD Movers* book for Columbia University in 2023. *The Bayou Bounce* is the 14th published children's book he has illustrated and designed. ■ Randell resides and works in Brooklyn, New York and is the CEO and Creative Director at Pearson Designs. ■

www.ingramcontent.com/pod-product-compliance
Lightning Source LLC
Chambersburg PA
CBHW040814120626

46547CB00004B/541